Communion of Asiago

Communion of Asiago

STEPHEN MURABITO

Communion of Asiago

Copyright © 2006
by Stephen Murabito

cover design by Trisha Hadley

All rights reserved. No part of this book may be used or reproduced in any manner whatsoever without written permission from the publisher, except in the case of brief quotations embodied in articles and reviews.

Published by

~Star Cloud Press~
6137 East Mescal Street
Scottsdale, Arizona 85254-5418

ISBN:
1-932842-17-9 — $14.95

Library of Congress Control Number: 2006921443

Printed in the United States of America

OTHER BOOKS BY STEPHEN MURABITO

Connections, Contexts, and Possibilities, Prentice Hall, 2001
[composition reader]

A Little Dinner Music, Parallel Press, 2004

The Oswego Fugues, Star Cloud Press, 2005

The Menu

INVOCATION

COMMUNION OF ASIAGO

Ethnic Poem
1

Grandma Zicci's Worst Nightmare
3

Salvatore Bucciagrossi Returns
5

The Kielbasa Ghosts
7

Traditions
9

New York Haiku: Ordering Corned Beef with Mayo
10

Little Louisiana Tabasco Hot Pepper
11

Sonny Rollins Dances with His Sax, and It Leads
13

All I Wanna Do: Oddly Holy at Wade's Diner
15

The Cook at Catalone's Loses His Mind
17

The Waitress
20

The Lost Digits of My Ancestors
24

The Bright Young Poets of America Twirl Spaghetti
and Beat It for the County Line
34

To Come Close
38

Alone with the Artichokes
41

To Fred and Jack: Poems for Pastries
43

The Nameless Breads
50

Bless You for Yesterday's Rolls
52

A Little Dinner Music
54

When We Danced this *Tarantella*
59

My Muse
62

Strawberry Jam as Cosmic Certainty
65

Communion of Asiago
69

BENEDICTION

How to Winter Out
73

These poems are for my wife, April.

From the first day that I beheld her face
   in this life till the vision of her now,
I could trust my poems to sing her praise.

          Dante Alighieri
          Paradiso XXX, 28-30
          Translated by Mark Musa

She peels the spuds. I clean the coffee pot.

"James, the salt," she says.

"Yes, m'lord, and the pepper besides," I say.

We are having a good time. It does not take much for a couple of hungry stiffs to have a good time. The spuds that begin to sizzle on the hot plate are enough. The pot that fills the room with its smell is enough.

Tom Kromer
Waiting for Nothing

INVOCATION

"But we two, sitting here in the shelter, eating and drinking,
Shall entertain each other, remembering and retelling [. . .]."

    Eumaios to Odysseus
    Homer's *Odyssey*
    15.398-99
    Translated by Richmond Lattimore

Oh, stranger, come, taste, hear, and see,
And don't be strange any more.
I've prepared a setting for you:
The everyday plates,
The muted earth tones,
The burnt oranges,
The deep reds and browns
And golds of hot bowls.
Come, the steam is rising
As I lift off these lids.
Yes, listen, for I have more
Than food to pass:
I have stories to tell—
Look, our reflections fill these plates
As a sleep of snow falls
Like apple blossoms
Over the bags of leaves.
I long to sing to you
Through all I've gathered.

Oh, it is good and fresh and warm.
Come, and bless me.
Sit, and tear
This hard-crusted bread.
It is all that I have,
The heart of my house,
Going deep to the blood.

Communion of Asiago

Ethnic Poem
~In Memory of My Grandparents~

> Perhaps the world will end at the kitchen table, while we are laughing and crying, eating of the last sweet bite.
>
> Joy Harjo
> "Perhaps the World Ends Here"

Here it comes
Through ruby glints
Of Uncle Leo's Chianti
And across the airspace
Inside this burning skull:
Bodies ascending stony Sicilian hillsides,
Spirits abundant as Catanian holy parades,
It's a flight, a flight: All of the lost relatives
Rise from the dead and fly now to the New World.
They are the songs of *pane*, Asiago, and olives on my breath!

Their hands shake, passion itself resurrecting their flesh.
They breathe Vivaldi through their eyes, exhale Dante in my ears.
And their children squirm with the small fires in their souls.
They're being held and told, *Hush, hush. Stay close, stay close.*
It's time now. We are returning, returning to his aching heart.

They want to cook and live and eat with their new friends;
They want to fill our faces with the blood of their smiles;
They want to touch us through the sauce and Romano we twirl
And twirl into yet another explosive dinner-table story.

Oh, let the world end; it'll begin again in bread as sweet as this
As they pass their lives into our veins, defy death, and sing,

Everyone, everyone, it's ready: Come, sit, eat, eat, eat!

Grandma Zicci's Worst Nightmare

Her yellow house is full,
And everyone is sitting, eating.

There are only the sounds of forks
Gracing plates, of glasses rising.

She's standing in her kitchen,
Defined by spent pots and pans.

Then someone comes running
Breathless on the tiled floor:

Nunzia! Nunzia! We're out of lasagna!
The fifty you baked were not enough!

Her eyes fill as she tells me this:
Santa Maria, Stefano. It's a sign.

I rip bread, slice the Provolone,
Pour her a short beer, and assure

Her that such passing horrors
Are merely the abominations of dream.

There is no patron saint of lasagna,
I joke, but she does not hear me

As the cheese breaks on her teeth,
Transforming her like the roses

That peer like children at her window.
She takes the bread and shakes it twice.

She nods, then bursts into story:
In a Sicilian home, she's a kid again

Cracking the sun, the sun, the sun
Of a dozen eggs into a flour well

Into the hours of hands of her grandmother
Into the perfect ribbons of fettuccine.

I fix a plate of olives, black as nightmares.
Sweetly, they disappear, one at a time.

Salvatore Bucciagrossi Returns

I am the famous "Professor."
I wail the blues on Bourbon Street,
And they run to interview me
When our plane lands in St. Louis.

I introduce my entourage
To the shining cameras:
Here's my wife, April.
There's E. J., my lead guitar . . .

Then someone asks, *But who's that man*
Wavering over your shoulder—
Him, in the red sweater and baggy brown pants—
The one holding the box of sausage casings,

With a meat grinder floating nearby?

And there is this heat
We share in our stomachs
And hearts as we turn to see
Salvatore Bucciagrossi,

The long-since-dead
Sausage maker from Oswego, NY.
The crowd yells my name.
The interviewers wait.

And someone accuses me of black magic.

But Salvatore Bucciagrossi baritones Bellini
To the Howlin' Wolf hush in our souls.
He embraces us all, saying he's risen
From his gravity to continue his work,

That he's come back from the dead
To protect me with salt, red pepper, and garlic,
To bless me with Sicilian hot sausage,
That this is God's single gift to me,

Which I should accept in the silence of fried onions.

The Kielbasa Ghosts

> Syracuse is losing two west side meat markets, the last in the city specializing in freshly made kielbasa and hams using age-old recipes brought over from the Old World.
>
> *Syracuse Post-Standard*
> May 1, 1997

> Polish kielbasa no longer hung in butchers' windows.
>
> Saul Bellow
> *Humboldt's Gift*

All across America,
The small Polish stores are closing
Down—no more kielbasa, sweet hams,
Kiszka, brown breads, or quarts
Of succulent beer
Inside the hard-sliding doors.

We are a blood-deep people:
Life doesn't simply hit us
And then fade away.
We love kielbasa; we're fighters.
And so, like a legion of the sleepwalking starved,
We will descend our porch
Steps and float out
To fill the early morning streets
With the wandering parts of ourselves
That will never rest.

Like flocks of wayward white eagles
In search of the skies and trees themselves,
We will fall on unsuspecting Polish festivals,
Razing the pierogi and golabki tables,
Inhaling the homemade kielbasa and kiszka,
Drinking in the cold beer
Until we are born again
In the spinning flesh and blood
And soul on a polka floor,

Where ghost on ghost
We refuse to leave,
Surrounding the son of a son
Of a son of a sausage maker,

Whirling like a crown above his head

Until he moves in the ticking sawdust quiet
Behind a Monday morning meat counter
To say hello to his first customer coming in,

The bells of a thousand tongues ringing at the door.

Traditions
~In Memory of John O'Brien~

I studied about the Indians—western ones.
God, if I didn't know everything there was.

I went to visit them: We ate chicken, drank
Everclear, danced, sang. They all broke up

When I rubbed chicken grease over my body.
Drunkenly, I explained myself: I believed

That it was a custom of theirs. I was mistaken.
Laughing, his arms around me, White Deer said

It wasn't really a custom of *theirs*, but maybe
They'd do it the *next time* they ate chicken.

New York Haiku: Ordering Corned Beef with Mayo

Sure, we'd serve it to them, but we'd make them eat it in the street!

        Anonymous Worker
        Carnegie Deli, New York City

The advice you'll get
In the more patient delis
Is *try* brown mustard.

They know that you're from
Kansas; they'll suggest again,
Try the brown mustard.

Yeah, sure, but

In certain New York
Delicatessens, just ask—
They'll shoot you on sight.

Little Louisiana Tabasco Hot Pepper
-For Jeff Schwartz, the Hot Pepper Man-

Little Louisiana Tabasco Hot Pepper:
I picture a brown-eyed southern belle
With just as much music to her name,
The eyelashes fluttering electric rushes
Through my soul, the hat broader
Than the breath I have to draw when
I see her. She leans back some to drink
Me in, and sighs, *Well now, hi there,
Stevie Joe! I'm Little Louisiana Tabasco
Hot Pepper!* And she kisses my face,
Her tongue hotter than faith, the insides
Of my mouth more alive than all of the sunshine
That has ever draped over her shoulders.

And Schwartz, the Hot Pepper Man tonight, wonders
If there's anything else he can get us to eat.
He says, *Have some hummus, hot with garlic.
It'll keep the flies off your face.* He says,
*Have another hot pepper. I eat them with eggs.
Here, try this green one. It's even hotter. Or maybe
Some horseradish. I grew it myself, out back!*

The heat! The wonderful heat of his face and stories
As he offers us every colorful thing in his house!
But no. I'm in love with my mind's hot lady. She knows
My tears are always hers, my prayers her pure flame.
Oh, she is the final lady, the one burning to me,

Here, one more baby toe, a last delicate kiss.
Consume me. Take my heart into your breath.

Sonny Rollins Dances with His Sax, and It Leads
~For Jack Giles~

Sonny Rollins comes walkin out
On stage, tall, gives a smile,
A nod, time in the shoulders,
Bobbin neck, breathes in, out,
Says, *Two*, shake, tap a foot,
Says, *One, two, three, four* . . .

And Sonny Rollins starts to blow:
He doesn't just *play* his sax,
He *dances* with it, and it leads:
In the knees, walkin, movin all
Over, a squint, a shudder, a grimace,
Turn it sideways, bend way over,

Give a skip, roll and weave, toes,
Heels, bop and sway like a possessed
Man with a bronzed broom: Sweep it up,
Lift it up high overhead to Godjazz up
Like a golden question mark blowin
The answers in runs, trills, blasts,

And shake it, shake it, flutter it
On home: Band windin on down, we're
All shoutin in the dark: Sound now solo,
Pure, street, nightbridge New York solo
With the band's last walk down the scale,
And song endin: Sonny, Sonny, Sonny Rollins:

Three squawkin rips to the last goosehonk toot.

All I Wanna Do: Oddly Holy at Wade's Diner

The brilliant orange ice
Of the sun rises
As I blow into my coffee
Here at Wade's Diner,
Where the toothless man in red flannel
Gums over his eggs,
And the aroma
Of the homemade raisin toast
Should be the last glorious inhalation
Of the living,
Our human salvation.

And I think of that generous woman
From down near Holland Patent
Who wouldn't tell me her name,
That magic, fluid one-night stand.
She kept saying with perfect sanity,
All I wanna do is love you.
That's all I wanna do.

She was an incredible rhythm
As I sang her all the blues I knew:
It was in cadenzas of her
Brown eyes, songs with mine.

We flung those "Lost Woman Blues"
Up, up from River Street,

The Oswego River riffing into Ontario.
Yeah, a rhythm to us by Vona's Shoes.
She was an angel of sexual release.

All I wanna do is hold you.
That's all I wanna do.

And then she was gone,
Just a spirit staying long enough
To buy me French toast
And watch me eat
And not stop smiling:

All I wanna do is feed you.
That's all I wanna do.

All of it
Oddly holy at Wade's Diner,
Like some kind of song
With roots in the breathy air,
Like all of the aromas
Becoming one aroma,
Like the grin
Behind the after-breakfast smoke—

Christ, like just the smoke itself.

The Cook at Catalone's Loses His Mind
(or, Pilgrimage with the Bronzed Jo Jo Annunziata Sausage Sandwich)

> Employees at Bongo Java, a coffee and pastry shop in Nashville, Tennessee, have "shellacked and enshrined" a cinnamon bun which bears a striking resemblance to Mother Theresa.
>
> Greensburg *Tribune-Review*
> December 29, 1996

At first, I thought, I'll be damned
If I make a pilgrimage to Nashville
To gaze at the face of Mother Theresa
Emerging from a shellacked cinnamon bun.

But then I heard a voice.
Maybe it was only Connie Angelucci,
Next door, cursing her husband:

Yes, you will be damned,
You heathen bastard!

But I don't know, though.
All night, I'm thinking about the timing.

Then I have this epiphany.
There must be hundreds of faces
In all of the foods we cook and eat,

But we're not stunned by them
Because they're not famous faces
Or even faces we know.

For example, maybe *my* face is on a veal scaloppini
Out in, say, Portland, Oregon.
Ok, I mean, Joe Schmoe there, he says,
Hey, Grace, looks like a face here in my scaloppini!
But he wouldn't recognize me,
So he eats the veal—no problem.

Then, guess what? I'm seeing faces everywhere:
Now, I've got a bronzed Jo Jo Annunziata sausage sandwich,
A laminated manicotti that looks
Like Celeste Desantis from on Sixth Street,
And a varnished dish of ziti and meatballs
That's the spitting image of Sister Marie,
My fifth grade catechism teacher,
Who used to pray the lessons at us, I swear,
Whispering us closer and closer
As the silent chalk blossomed
Into words on the old blackboard.

I've even shellacked a gnocchi and pork chops
That looks like Connie Angelucci herself,
God bless her with the fat on her arms
Bouncing all over as she's pulling her husband
Onto the dance floor this Saturday night
When Augie Augustine and the Gents are playing.

Oh, bless them all,
Out there twirling, laughing,
Their faces turning to rigatoni,
Linguine, cacciatore,

Or the sweet, succulent shrimp scampi.

The Waitress
~For Joey, Mary Jane, and All of the Girls at Vona's~

This is to the patron saint of waitresses.
Your name is Charlene
Or Darlene or Marlene—we can't tell
As the first letters of your name tag
Are worn away
Into your white collar,
And the beat-up pen angles
Outside your thin pocket
Holding the back-up order pad.

We raise our glasses to you,
Your shoes worn through,
The uniform stiff, fresh,
Peach or sky blue, off-yellow or classic black—
We can't tell as lights dim, and we meditate or pray,
Your lips about to speak,
Would you like to see a menu?
Can I take your order?
Would you like something from the bar?
Is everything all right?

Your face is a bronzed glowing,
Yet the sunken cheek in the shifting light.
The artist has captured
Your infinite patience,

The resiliency of the natural rhythm
Of lifting a freshly brewed pot of coffee
Without losing a single note
Or tipping the circus act
Of plates in your other hand.

All those who doubted you
Before, now know your miracles:

First, dinner shift done,
The girls driving in Linda's Toronado,
You rose above the gravity
Of humming foot and leg pain
For that one split second
Of hope and forgetting
As the first Marlboro
Tasted like God
On the way to Thirsty's Place,
Where maybe there'd be a band,
And you told your "fig-plucker" joke,
The Olds resurrected with laughter.

Second, the night frozen pork chops
Came down like kung fu weaponry
On McKenzie's head
As he cornered you fat-fingered

In the walk-in freezer,
Beef bones sticking into your back.

He pressed into you, said,
I been lovin' your tits for five years, honey.
There was blood,
Just a tiny Allegheny of it
Snaking down his forehead—
Blood but never a word again
Through those browned teeth.

And third, the morning
That broke through the blinds
Too early that one day—
You pick a day—
When you woke up but couldn't look
Into the empty room

Or into the mirror,
But got washed and dressed anyway
And moved with Olympic strength
Down the steps
To catch the 54C
Up Carlisle to Craig,
Transferring at Norton,

All the streets becoming men
Worked into your tired blood:
Oh, all of the dreamy boyfriends
Strong enough to hold your life.

And, miracle of miracles,
You crossed Dante Street,
Headed for the back doors,
Strode through the aroma of fresh coffee,
Grabbed a pen and a new pad,
Wrote down the names of the specials,
Hit the floor smiling,
Greeted the party of five,

And took your first order of the night.

The Lost Digits of My Ancestors
~For Ed Ochester~

I

Uncle Tony P. was brave
Around the cans of anchovies—
What the hell?
He had nothing to lose,
Having already lost most
Of his fingers a digit at a time
Down at Imperial Wire.

Inside their closet,
I found his bowling ball
And held the crooked grin of holes
While he made us an antepasti.

Aunt Mayme
Shouted his last name,
But it was useless
Because he was half-deaf.

She yelled each syllable:
Pa eee no! Pa eee no!
She cried the salty, rich food
Would surely make me sick.

But he hummed Sinatra,
Chomped his White Owl,
And mixed the anchovies,
Capers, salami, peppers,
And black olives together.

I sat and smiled
And felt whole
With a hunk of Provolone
In the small kitchen,
All yellow
And a pink flamingo out back.

I copied him,
Reaching as he reached,
Tearing and dipping bread
As he tore and dipped it.
And our bellies buldged
As he clawed out
The oily, sweet seconds.

II

Cousin Monk
Pulled Billy McGuire
Out of the Presser
Down at Whitlock Shadecloth,

Pulled him
Right out of his clothes—
Set him bare-assed
On the concrete floor.

Monk said
Billy wept
And bled
And swore
All shaky
That he saw Jesus
Sittin' on the bolts
Of new cloth.

Monk lost three
Digits on two
Fingers of his left hand
And lost the tip
Of his right
Forefinger.

He said they popped
Off like corks.

He lifted us up
High off the ground

But then left the room
On Thanksgiving
When Uncle Angelo
Opened the Burgundy.

People looked and looked,
But not even Maintenance
Found those digits.

III

Aunt Yolanda was tipsy
At the family reunion.
We were steaming clams
And grilling sweet sausage.
She was a live wire.

Uncle Willy bossed her around.
She stood up in the shady yard,
Told him to eat shit,
Said she'd been his cookin' slave
So long that she could do
A damned travellin' magic show.

I laughed so hard
That salad fell
Into my lap,
And oil and vinegar and piss
Ran down my leg
And over my sneaks.

But he took her up on it,
Bet her twenty bucks
There and then
She couldn't chop that lemon
Into two perfect halves.

Like some crazy pirate lady,
She raised that curving blade,
And before I knew it,
They were all off
And yelling their ways
Down the hill
To the hospital.

But with her waving anger
And spitting Italian,
She'd tossed the half-thumb
Out the Buick window,
And they were all
On their knees
By Dinkie's Mobil,

In front,
In the weeds,
Searching.

IV

My father moved slowly
Over the fresh sawdust.
His fingers were red,
Always red: He'd been
Boning-out pork all night.

I soaked the salty ropes
Of hog casings in water.
I threw a little worm of it
To the purring cat.

Soon, the fresh sausage
Wound to life in his hands,
Curling in the pans.

But my *Playboy* girlfriend
With her raised skirt
Would understand the lump
In my throat.
Her breasts like melons,
Her eyes like chestnuts,

Down in that basement,
She came to life—
Flesh on the flashlight pages.

The happy grinding behind me,
I creaked down the stairs.
These magazines
And women
All opening,
And God:
Imagine
The world
Is so damned big
That *this* is
Going on somewhere.

Through the smile
Of my girl
Offering a light
For my candy Camel,
There shot the cry—
High-pitched like brakes.
They had to put him out
And amputate,
Cutting the digits
Clean at the joints.

V

Tonight, in Pittsburgh,
The talk is
Some school kid
Down on Atwood
Found a hand
In the snow.

I don't know why,
But it seems like
I've grabbed my bourbon before
And followed the same crowd.

The cops send us home.

And everyone's wondering
Where on earth
The lost hand came from.

Someone says, *Mafia.*
Someone says, *Maniac.*

I chug my booze
And cling to the air.
I burst to Mrs. Pasquale
That all the way from my hometown,
Down through the old wires overhead

And the bowling balls and buried weeds
And the lemons and sausage
And pots and pans
Of all the houses
In this city,
The lost digits
Of my ancestors
Have come together
As a hand that reaches
Out for me, reaches.

My wife makes my apologies,
And Mrs. Pasquale simply says,
That's ok, honey. Sometimes
It's the little things in life
That upset some of us.
Don't worry, sweetie.

You're getting too old
For that kind of shit!
My wife's breath clouds, fades.

I sit on the porch,
Watch the snow fall,
Drink the warm bourbon,
And feel myself
Turning forty.

But they are all dead,
Those leaving unwhole,
And their digits
Have been relegated
To the places of the lost,
The scattered
And wandering
Endless shards of the world,
Crowded, weeded, and snowed-over,

Whiskey breath
And memory
And oil cans
In the lots
And this back alley,

Where one hand
Holds another
On a Tuesday night,
And no one else
In Pittsburgh
Is praying.

The Bright Young Poets of America Twirl Spaghetti and Beat It for the County Line

> "Remove yourselves," Giuseppe cried. "Man needs spaghetti!"
>
> > Pietro Di Donato
> > *Christ in Concrete*
>
> The official poems read over
> the loudspeakers
> were particularly mediocre. Art
> was confounded no end;
> verse, for the moment, was hushed.
>
> > Thomas Merton
> > "From the Second Chapter of Verse History of the World"

In the next century,
After some charismatic president
Quotes Plato in a stirring oration,
All of America will begin reading the dialogues
And then *The Republic*
And think themselves smart,
A little too smart after "Book X":
Cities, townships, small hamlets,
Influenced by such lunacy,
Will begin the ban of poetry and poets.

Books will burn.
Bodies will break.

The average man or woman,
Previously anyone's mother or father,
Will be hysterically
Quoting and misquoting Socrates,
And ignorant belief may win the day.

However, the bright young poets of America
Will not listen, saying as one,
It's all rhetorical.

And at one of the God-awful rallies,
A mother or father will rant over a bullhorn,
Trying now a few strategies of his or her own,
Telling the bright young poets of America
That poetry isn't real, isn't cash,
And only means sorrow, pain,
Hunger, starvation, and death.

Not to worry, though.
Despite my great age,
I'll be there in force.

I'll sprout up
From under the speaker's table
Like an uncontrollable yeast reaction,
Like an unwanted Mediterranean hard-on
At an English tea party.

And I'll be living textual proof
That poets don't starve or die.
I'll shake in my old boots,
And somehow the simple will become magic:
A narrative whose heart is a tuna noodle casserole,
A dramatic uniting with two goblets of Koolaid,
A lyric chanting the trochees of a midnight pancake supper.
I'll give a litany of bread, wine, and salt,
The simple peace raised in the light of human kitchens.
But most of all, I'll chant for spaghetti,
The ultimate form in the macaronic prosody of life:

>   *Any sauce'll do—some lucky clams*
>   *With oil and a clove of garlic!*
>   *These things, these things, damn it,*
>   *These things feed your souls!*

Seeing how poetry is *not*
At removes from reality,
Their mouths and minds watering,
The chains of cash broken at last,
The bright young poets of America will follow me,
And we'll beat it for the county line,
Where seeming meets being every time.

However, Mom and Dad
And the Platonic hometown
Won't take this sitting down.

They've heard of me and my kind
In our station wagons, rusted Continentals,
And patriotic pickup trucks.

And as we ride off,
I'll teach the bright young poets of America
That all dialectics begin
Between forks and spoons.
And the bright young poets of America
Will twirl
With the ease
Of old Ben Jonson
Consumed in iambs and anapests.

But then I'll see that wall of light,
State Troopers
Between us and the future of truth.
And every last spaghetti pound of me
Will slam down hard onto the gas,
And I'll sing my final song:

> *Keep your heads down,*
> *And twirl low—*
> *Those bastards've got shotguns!*

To Come Close
~For Gerald Stern~

Here we are,
In his poem,
In Europe,
That's fine,
A place for fresh escargot—
I don't mind garlic that early,
Fresh escargot and green grapes:
God is made of fresh escargot and green grapes.

And the smell of the wine
Is lingering on my words—
The sleep, the death,
The dream of such a life
That's left in the waking eye.

And writing ten lines a day.
Stern tells us at Pitt
That he strove in France to write ten lines a day.
Listen to me calling him Stern—
Oh, for Christ's sake,
That's all right with me
If it's all right with him,
And it seems to be as he spits on us,
His words still full of Iron City.
Yes, I could live for ten lines a day.

Now, it's France,
And the old woman
Emerges with her magic
Breads and cheeses.
She is staring down at me
On my knees
Under the bushes
Tangled in the vines,
And she's wondering why
I am inhaling the earth.

And I can't tell her
That I am trying to write
Ten lines a day,
That I am someone
Listening, waiting,
But always waking
Up in the vines
To the acrid smell of weeds,
And privy to a stranger's
Sour Pittsburgh nightmares.

And the old woman draws close,
Wearing the smile of her life—
Flesh and round kindness—
A light to absorb my confusion.
She tells me to rise,
To eat the fish, the cheese, the bread,

To sip the nice Beaujolais,
Life's ruby from green,
That God is made of ruby from green,
That these, *these* are my ten lines a day.

And in the Pittsburgh night swelter
Of blacktop, sirens, and brick alleys,
I sit with April, who is summer dress,
Jug wine, and smiles,
And we share the last
Of the New York cheddar,
And bread breaks with idea,
Breaks now with flake of cooling lemon cod
And splinter of light that is God, too:

    Look out the window!
    The berries are as black as peppercorns!
    The words are rounder than grapes!
    I am an old man singing a song of fish,
    Snails, bread, cheese, and resurrection!
    To come close! To come close! To come close!
    To live the words you breathe and sing again:
    Flesh, woman, day, night, and wineman in the vines!
    I'll wake and revise my unfinished Hercules poem:
    Oh, on his knees, he'll beg the gods for mortality.

Alone with the Artichokes

I can't believe that of all things
It's me and these artichokes in the dark,
No early morning light, no last-minute

Preparations, April's anxious hands
Tucking the tin foil around the rim.
No, these leftover artichokes soak,

The oil separating into small pools
Like sparkling glasses of Galliano.
The vinegar coils into red pockets

Of bitterness that sting the tongue
Like the memory of sour words.
I can't believe that I've taken

The lion's share of everything
From everyone in my entire life,
But that's what she said.

Yes, I forgot April's birthday party
And went to a clambake in Fulton,
Eating all day with pumpkin-gutted men.

Drinking Molson drafts, I forgot the whole thing.
The minutes became dozens of oysters,
Shrimp, clams, friends with our bullshit stories.

And all day, she waited here for me,
Moving in this darkening kitchen,
Stirring these quartered, soaking hearts.

To Fred and Jack: Poems for Pastries
~For Jack Harper, and in Memory of Fred Bishop~

> I cried for flour, and meat, I declare, it was strong.
> Well, I cried for flour, and meat, I declare, it was strong.
> Keep a feeding me cornbread, I just can't stick around long.
>
> Blind Lemon Jefferson
> "Rabbit Foot Blues"

I've spent all my money
To come to graduate school.
I said, I spent all my good money
Just to come to this graduate school.
And tonight
My stomach hardens
Like some peach pit
In the gut of a fool.

But Fred and Jack lean close, swig their Gennies, and say,
Aw, come on now, Stevie, a little personal hunger? It'll go away!
Spiritual hunger, intellectual starvation—now, that's a problem!
Here, have some unnamable cheese, drink this undrinkable wine!
They've dragged me to an ecology conference at SUNY Oswego,
Where a speaker concludes, *There's a new harmony on the planet.*
Then the host asks, *So, are there any questions or responses?*
Jack, a 350-pound rhododendron nurseryman, puts his arms
Around us and announces that our—that's right, *our*—
Response/question will be delivered in sarcastic mime

By brilliant Fred, who is finishing his PhD in Philosophy.
Fred begins to beat a toy stuffed-seal with a wiffleball bat.
Silence. Here comes a woman, red-faced, her fists actually up.
God, it looks like Marciano in drag hammering a librarian.

Jack turns to me: *I believe we've made our point, don't you?*
Fred's on the floor, a Beetle Bailey with a crumpled bat,
His humor in a twisted heap of defeated theory.
As we are tossed out to the applause (some for, some against),
The host howls, *The only reason you aren't under arrest is*
That this is a college, and we must tolerate such outbursts!
To which I reply, *The only reason you write empirically is*
That you are data-driven and cannot comprehend implication!
Outside in the snow, we celebrate with new Gennies and old Triscu
We discuss the human failure to understand the seriousness of come
At the Clam Bar, we try to explain Fred's cuts to his squinting wife,
But we can't. We do a bear dance showing the lack of universal harr
Oh, they buy us burgers and beer, and we are one with our fine expr

Fact is,
I live on it.
Fred, Jack,
I haven't eaten
In a week.
And my head sinks
Into all this composition theory.
I said, my head sinks
Into all this composition theory.

Why does so much knowledge
Got to be so damned dreary?

But like maddening ideas refusing to die,
We are loose again on the streets of Oswego.
Bar to bar, we take our Aristotles, our Homers,
Our Einsteins through dialectics of black and tans.
At last, Little Lil kicks us out of her place.
We head down to the greasy spoon on West First,
And I am an old Celtic poet transformed
Into the contortions of a drunken blues singer.
I wail among the lost of the last call,
The lonely on their stools, knee-deep in home fries.

> *My baby's a needle,*
> *And I'm her sweet thread.*
> *She likes how I push her,*
> *And I like how I'm led.*

> *We sew lots of patches.*
> *We sew like little fools.*
> *We sew 'til there's nothin'*
> *But all these empty spools.*

My baby gets tired,
And I start to wilt.
But one day, now, mister,
We'll make us a quilt.

'Cause my baby's a needle,
And I'm her little thread.
She likes how I push her,
And I like how I'm led.

And soon, everyone, everyone is laughing and clapping.
And my harmonica, my harmonica: God, I can blow
The color out of dripping egg yolks sunnyside up.
Blow, blow, blow, I'm a chorus of mumbled obscenities.
And I'm dancing with the miraculous waitress
Who does a three-plate pirouette to thunderous applause.
Howling people throw tips in my cloudy milk glass,
And I feel my happy heart in its 1-4-5 progression,
The mounds of food we never eat going cold, greasy, limp.

The mounds of food we never eat going cold, greasy, limp.

Or
Is the world
Eating me,
Never knowing
My face,
Humor, or song?

I said, or
Is the world
Eating me,
Never knowing
My face,
Humor, or song?

I've come a long way since sun-up,
But, baby, the way is still so damned long.

But here we come, charging into the Super Duper market,
The late-night clerk's face like a round rhubarb pie.
There's no arguing with a 350-pound rhododendron nurseryman
Proposing an intriguing value system of culinary aesthetics:
We will do poems for pastries, Jack shouts like a royal ringmaster
Transposed into the bakery section, *Poems for pastries!*
The breadstick he hands me becomes the Ollambh's staff:

> *I'll give you a double sestina*
> *For six strawberry strudels,*
> *A voluptuous villanelle for vanilla tarts,*
> *A couple of couplets for a caramel cream crunch!*
>
> *I'll give you trochees for tortes,*
> *Dramatics for date bars,*
> *Lyrics for a lemon magnifico!*
> *Or I'll wail hard-wrought spondees*
> *For a dozen polka-dot waffles!*

The hysterical clerk hands us boxes and boxes of old pastries.
We choke them down and toss them up into the red Oswego sunri
They are maple hockey pucks over the icy parking lot.
They are sugar-glazed parking tickets under windshield wipers.
They are, somehow, the perfect expression of our existence.
And as the streetlights go out, we are three blind men-children
On our knees with a stale cheesecake, reinventing the wheel.

Turning,
Turning,
My Pittsburgh
Mind and stomach
Rise and fall
Like Ontario waves
In an Oswego daybreak.
Ah, an Oswego daybreak:
That place was breathing song.

This place
Is a good place
But oh, *not* a place
Of poems for pastries.

Fred, Jack, I haven't searched the ground
For small change since I was five.

I said, I haven't searched the ground
For small change since I was five.

It's been a long, long, time, now, baby,
Since I laughed until I cried.

The Nameless Breads
*~In Memory of Uncle Ralph, and the
Bygone White Eagle Bakery, Rome, NY~*

We're home now from Saint Luke's Hospital,
Where in his two exhausted tongues,
Uncle Ralph had asked us all to let him die.
He said it first in thickened, careful English
As if we would see to his polite request.
He sighed it again in soft, defeated Polish.
An immigrant was brought in to translate:
Ralph says he's old and tired. He's ready now.
We nodded, pretending it was news to us.

Now, we stand in Cousin Frannie's kitchen,
Her house replete with the sweet emergence
Of ham and salads, whiskey, beer, and smoke.
We eat and talk, recover in his stories.
It's Christmas. There are children running,
Cries and laughter fusing toward one voice.
Aunt Julie sends me down the street for bread.

And I know I don't speak a word of Polish
As I step inside White Eagle Bakery.
I remember the trips down here with Ralph.
He'd point to rolls and kinds of bread, then breathe
Their names as if they were his children.

And I want life to metamorphose from
The current happy customers to me.
They speak their private Polish—hard yet still
A graceful music, heavy with whispered love.
And the golden *babka* Christmas breads
Sit on the counter like gigantic plumes
Of God. I search my mind for the Polish
That Ralph taught me, but my tongue won't move.
It's my turn, but the words die in my mouth.

The owner waits on me then goes out back.
And now, the place is empty: My arms
Are heavy with the miracle of bread.
It's everything and nothing I can name,
A smell in the heart as racks of new loaves
Are wheeled out for the Christmas rush,
And I'm surrounded by all the breads,
All the breads, Uncle Ralph—the nameless breads.

Bless You for Yesterday's Rolls
~In Memory of the Kunst Bakery, Pittsburgh, PA~

Imagine me,
You beautiful German bakeshop goddess you!

Imagine me,
You Friday afternoon flour-handed wonderment you!

Oh, how about me,
Tossing you the quarters I owe for yesterday's rolls!

Bless you! Bless you! Bless your day-old bread and round kindness!

Yes, it's me,
My face no longer longer than a front-page tragedy!

Yes, it's me,
Telling you to keep the change from a loaf of round rye, too!

     How about us, now,
Payday among the pies and pastries,
Where you can't meet my eyes,
Where part of me will remember you forever,
Arms and hands and cakes and tortes,
Where I leave, and you let
That baker's smile break to me at last
As you wave me out the door.

        How about me, now,
The living dream of bread,
A glow up Meyran Avenue
As I turn the corner to see you
Loving string around another white box,
As I walk further into the everyday, into the fresh snow,
The weight of caring warming my hands,
As I take your life's work home with me,

As I eat and read, and you laugh and bake.

A Little Dinner Music

> Music is feeling, then, not sound [. . .]
>
> Wallace Stevens
> "Peter Quince at the Clavier"

I

April finishes her make-up
Under the big Bartlett tree.
My father puts the hedge trimmers away
And calls for a two-beer lunch.

We've spent the morning pruning
The Red Delicious, the Rome,
The older Cortland trees.
So happy to be out of Pittsburgh,
April and I danced
Backwards again and again,
Stopping, turning, gaining perspective.

And I tangoed with a rake,
Working through the crisp McIntosh:
They were old fists, imperfect
As the shady orchard itself
With its patches of burnt grass,
Its twisted lines of branch shadows.
And in my upstate frenzy,

Breathing Hesperides in the apple air,
I didn't care that my fingers blistered
Or that my hands stung
Like the half-ripe Granny Smith
I couldn't help biting into.

II

The tomatoes have been late this year,
But so have we: We're lucky
To make it to Oswego in August,
To pick our lunch from the garden,
Waltzing the small basket of ripeness
To the kitchen cutting board.

I chop and assemble
With the Dutch College Swing Band.
Cucumber, radish, celery:
Charlie Parker blows fresh garlic to pieces.
Lettuce, tomato, fresh basil:
Oil and vinegar glisten
Like the sweat on the faces of the dancers
Who bop and twirl to Turk Murphy,
Live from the only
Red-carpeted saloon in San Francisco!

A little dinner music, my father says,
Turning up the stereo.
He layers Provolone, Genoa, copicolla.
The hot mustard is spread a little faster,
The knife tapping the bread.
My salad finally arrives
Like something blossoming
To Louis Armstrong's gargled joy
Of "Bourbon Street Parade."

You eat lunch like this all of the time? I ask
But he's promising April
The first dance after the second beer,
And I don't ask again.

The soppressata blesses us.
We savor Dina Washington's "Unforgettable."

Then he squints, points, and praises,
Hey, Stevie—the Duke, Duke Ellington.

The olives become oiled jewels.
The old Apollo Theatre rises like the phoenix.

III

After lunch, we sit in the parlor.
My father sleeps through Anita O'Day,
Eddie Condon, and Woody Herman.

But I picture tomorrow's breakfast:
He'll show us Wild Bill Davison trumpeting
The sun into the steam of our coffee.

April takes my hand,
And we dance to Gerry Mulligan.

Artie Shaw, Oscar Peterson,
And we dip in love by the front door.

Miles Davis,
Someone blows "Twelfth Street Rag,"
And we do "The Kansas City Stomp"
Under the big Bartlett tree.

And through the bay window,
We can see my father,
The gray head falling further,
The hands unwinding into sleep.

And only if we're silent,
Beyond our descending breath
And the empty, stretching Hall Road,
Can we hear at last
The slightest guitar or clarinet

Like something imagined
Across a great distance
Coming finally to us

As another song begins.

When We Danced this *Tarantella*
~For April~

We followed digestion to bed,
Taking the French suggestion for love to heart

That first night we made love,
A cook and a waitress
Home after the Christmas party—
Gifts and bowls of food in paper bags,
Breath of bourbon, wine, salty anchovy.

We threw ourselves
Into ourselves
Toward something else:

We fell onto the floor
And were as hot and sloppy
As fresh eggplant parmesan
Sliding off of a plate.

And after,
While you slept,
I knew I loved you,
Your face framed in auburn curls,
Glowing like a Provolone in *groceria* moonlight,
Your uniform and worn shoes
Spent like a pile of onion shucks.

I gave your body
The jewelry of food.
I took the stems from fresh mushrooms
And placed the caps over your nipples.
I gave you God's brooch,
A bulb of garlic.
In your navel,
I put one green grape.

And bending toward you,
My buffet,
I took the green grape between my teeth
And somehow thought of Pappas,
My Greek college friend,
Who professed the calisthenics of love,

How he said all I had to do was practice
Rolling grapes over my teeth
Without breaking the skin,
And, oh, I could suck a girl's breasts
Until she melted like butter in the sun.

I bit the grape.

One bead of juice
Disappeared into your stomach,
Into my sleeping hope
That when we made our children,

I would want them to know
That yes, there was a time
When we lived like this,
When we danced this *tarantella*
Of garlic breath
And mushroom breasts
And green grapes rising.

My Muse
~After Ed Ochester and David Wagoner~

Magnificent in the echoing kitchen,
After all the scaloppini and cacciatore,

The manicotti, the ziti, and the fried fish specials,
My muse says, *Olympus? That sounds Greek*—

And words against stacks of cleaned pots and pans,
She's off, telling me about the Zavolos family,

How they had her over Sundays for lamb,
How Mrs. Zavolos crafted the rich baklava,

But how the youngest boy, Freddy, was wild
With the girls and broke his mother's heart

To death the night they arrested him
Inside Doyle's Camera Shop downtown.

My muse turns up the one burner, her hands
Never still, hot peppers dancing in oil and garlic,

Her voice meshing with the sizzling pan
But disappearing into the droning fan:

*Honey, there are cold Gennies in the fridge.
There's bread. I sliced it fresh just now.*

*And look, I bought you a few nice cigars,
But try not to smoke too much, ok?*

My muse never sits. She leans, humming
Against the warming table, watching me eat.

Bread, peppers, sausage, linguine, beer: Her
Rhythm, color, and art bloom on the plate.

Under the lamps, she spreads out my newest poems,
Whispering words into the stacks of serving dishes.

This is her gift to me, and I love the grease stains
Fingerprinting each page she's held. Carefully,

My muse puts three pencils in my pocket
And places a tomato and olive salad on top

Of the folded poems: *These are good. Now, eat.*
Then the one piece of ricotta cheesecake.

*I been worrying over it all day, Stevie.
I couldn't get the fresh cream from Taylor's,*

And that damned oven still ain't right, I swear.
But each bite is proof on the tongue that songs

Exist beyond our hearing, that beauty shall never
Let us know or name her completely,

That we need a language we don't yet own
To name ourselves dumb before dream and time.

Finally, the last ancient pot hung to dry,
She sits and sips the cold Gennie draft

That Tommy and Murph send back from the bar.
Those are good pencils, she says. *Wear them down.*

And that's all she says. As I leave, she has
Her one smoke before I know she'll get up,

Nod over her kitchen, and turn to hit the lights.

Strawberry Jam as Cosmic Certainty
~In Memory of My Mother, Helen Zoni Murabito~

> Walking in the autumn woods do you feel that a subtle distance has come between you and the smell of wood smoke? Have you drafted your obituary? Are you easily winded? Do you wear a girdle? Is your sense of smell fading, is your interest in gardening waning, is your fear of heights increasing [. . .]?
>
> John Cheever
> "The Death of Justina"

When they're rejecting
Everything you've done,
And they don't even like your face
In their archways any more;

When they've done their best,
And, God knows, it is *nearly* good enough,
To convince you that all
You've ever held true is, ultimately, simply *plain wrong*;

When the world begins
This descent into unknowable fragments,
Do one favor for me,
And say, *Bullshit!*

Fashion it through
The various rooms of your house
Until you begin to smile,

And the color returns to your face,
Your eyes, my friend.

And then, at last,
Stand on your back porch,
And burst it all the way out to the irises.
Only this time,
Use a strong Polish accent—
Like this, *Bullshit!*

Oh, enjoy that guttural explosion
That happens when the two *l's*
Are worked over, embraced,
Occupying more than your throat
Seems capable of holding
Seconds before the powerful *sh*-sound
Fires through your teeth
Toward the happy finality
Of the ever-ascending *it*.

Bullshit!

Say it, say it, say it, my good friend,
And mean every redemptive,
Cardio-vascular-rehab syllable of it,
Every musical exhalation of it,
And tell them

That you were given this gift
Wrapped around a jar
Of my mother's Oswego County strawberry jam.

Tell them she lost her leg
And nearly her life
And then came back to get carried away
With the idea of making, making, making
One upstate New York afternoon
And produced twenty-some jars of the stuff.

And when my father came home and asked,
Hey, Helen, what the hell gives with all this jam?
She said, *Ah, shut up!*
Yet under her breath,
She whispered something more,
Some words we'll never know for sure,
But we swore we heard, *Bullshit!*

Tell them that there is one absolute certainty,
Real and heavy and thick and sweet,
Triple-wrapped, and taped some more
In a whole damned newspaper,
And then rolled inside an old paper bag
Because it is one of life's mysteries
That this is the only way it can be delivered.
And then tell them that there is
This Polish-American lady somewhere

Now—yes, *now* as we speak—
Telling her husband to kiss off
As she makes too much strawberry jam
Yet still finds a home for every jar.

They sit on porch swings.
They wait in mailboxes.
They keep time beside evening editions.

Look, there are two now.
They are resting on the small table
Inside the back door
Of Josie Loschiavo's place,
Where word was she had the blues.

Communion of Asiago

> For the olive
> will sing with the wine:
> the ripening light will inhabit us.
>
> Pablo Neruda
> "In Praise of Oil"
> Translated by Ben Bellitt

This fig will save you

If you close your tired eyes
As you pull the Kalamata
From its hemp string.

Time stops in your palm.

Understanding is the light,
Ageless aroma under the cellophane.
It grows to certainty
With the explosion of sweetness

That says, *earth, sun, tree, hand, mouth.*

I've been taught the grace of eggplant,
The salvation of olives, the epiphany of garlic.
I have had lessons
In the redemption of plum tomatoes.

When I was seven, Grandpa Joe
Sat me down at his kitchen table
And desperately whispered,
This isa what I wait to show you.
This isa for your whole life.

He pulled a package
From his locked tackle box:
Strong string crossed tight
White butcher paper. Inside it,
A pungent slab of Asiago pulsed with light.
Louie Cordino smuggled it from Syracuse
Because my grandmother had gotten
To every local grocer, and not even my
Father was allowed to give him the cheese,
Genoa, or prosciutto he loved.

Oh, this lunatic is always before me—
His old knife, and the way
The backlit slice falls
Onto his thick fingers.

In his eyes, though, I saw
The treasure of teaching.
He gestured and said, *Ah? Ah?*
As if we were in a presence
As obvious as it was holy.

I saw the depths of ten seconds as he checked
Back toward the sewing room for Grandma,
Nodding in his own certainty,
Eyes now brown pure joyful saved
Then shutting at the bite
That said, *home, mother, father, son, grandson.*
I swore he was asleep.

Oh, the world tore itself to shreds, ignoring the wordless
Time of white crumbs on a stilled blade,
The endless patience of five sardines on a white plate,
Or the utter omniscience of fresh bread,
Which he tore and blessed with Tuscan oil.

His steady hand gave me the communion
Of Asiago in that human kitchen,
Where, a year later, my widowed grandmother wept
She'd forgotten her sauce recipe.
To an Italian, this is to lose your name.

But on the next day,
He was caught again,
And I stood watching the mortal sin
Of an old woman burying his infinite
Wisdom behind a line of rosebushes
As if the thorny arms
Could keep such dreams away.

Oh, the transcendence of Sicilian black olives,
The forgiveness of fettuccine,
The peace of Bardolino in the chipped glass:
This is all the mercy we have against
Sorrow, gravity, pain, damnation, and death.

Let the fig save you.
Pour the reconciliation of oil.
Fry the time of peppers.
Crush the days of garlic.
Slice the lives of cheese.
Break the soul of bread.

Hold each until song breaks clear.

Close your eyes.

Open your mouth.

Sip this wine.

Ascend.

BENEDICTION: How to Winter Out
~After Patricia Dobler's "Wintering Out"~

Do not hide
In the cellar
Regardless of your beer supply
Value the blackbird
Without it
The robin's song falls flat
Burn the wood
And sing the blues
And let the pork roast cook
On the old iron stove
All day long
Eat garlic
And breathe poetry
Into your lover's face
And thereby open yourself
To the rare sun
Don't look when it goes down
Remember
Let all voices wait
And all flesh be silence
And all flame be a language
Perfectly understood
Yet constantly in need
Of such translation

Acknowledgments

I thank the editors and readers of the following periodicals, where these poems first appeared (some in slightly different forms): "Invocation," *Tara's Literary Arts Journal*; "Ethnic Poem," *Antietam Review*; "The Kielbasa Ghosts," "All I Wanna Do: Oddly Holy at Wade's Diner," and "The Cook at Catalone's Loses His Mind," *5AM*; "Salvatore Bucciagrossi Returns," *Chiron Review*; "Traditions," *Minnesota Review*; "Little Louisiana Tabasco Hot Pepper," *Pig Iron*; "Sonny Rollins Dances with His Sax, and It Leads," *Cadence: The American Review of Jazz and Blues*; "The Lost Digits of My Ancestors," *Beloit Poetry Journal*; "The Bright Young Poets of America Twirl Spaghetti...," *Phoenix*; "To Come Close" and "Alone with the Artichokes," *Tar River Poetry*; "Bless You for Yesterday's Rolls," *Mississippi Review*; "A Little Dinner Music," *Long Pond Review*; "When We Danced this Tarantella," *Laurel Review*; "My Muse," *Pittsburgh Quarterly On-Line*; "Communion of Asiago," *Loyalhanna Review*; and "Benediction: How to Winter Out," *Pitt Magazine*. "Benediction..." also appears in *The Autumn House Anthology of American Poems and Prayers*, edited by Robert Strong (Autumn House Press, 2007).

I also thank Jan Beatty, host of the WYEP (Pittsburgh) radio show *Prosody*, for having me on to read these poems in 2004; and Frank Correnti, editor of *Pittsburgh Quarterly*, for having me read them for Radio Services for the Blind in 1999. And for their ceaseless support of my work, I am especially thankful to Ed Ochester, Judith Vollmer, and Richard Blevins—each one in his or her own way *"il miglior fabbro."*

This book was completed under the auspices of a grant from the National Endowment for the Arts.

STEPHEN MURABITO is an associate professor of English at the University of Pittsburgh's Greensburg campus. He has been an NEA Fellow in Poetry, and his poems have appeared in such places as *Beloit Poetry Journal*, *Mississippi Review*, and *5AM*. His chapbook, *A Little Dinner Music*, was published by Parallel Press in 2004, and his book-length poem, *The Oswego Fugues*, came out from Star Cloud Press in 2005. His short stories have appeared in such places as *North American Review*, *Antietam Review*, and *Paper Street*, and he is also the editor of the composition textbook *Connections, Contexts, and Possibilities* (Prentice Hall, 2001). He lives in Saltsburg, Pennsylvania, with his wife, April, and their four children Angelina, Estella, Antonia, and Sebastian.

CPSIA information can be obtained
at www.ICGtesting.com
Printed in the USA
LVHW091736221220
674907LV00004B/809